EUCHARISTIC APOSTLES
OF
THE DIVINE MERCY

CENACLE FORMATION
MANUAL III

Eucharistic Apostles of The Divine Mercy

Cenacle Formation Manual III

Bryan and Susan Thatcher

Marian Fathers of The Immaculate Conception
Stockbridge, Massachusetts 01263
2014

Available from:
Marian Helpers Center
Stockbridge, MA 01263

Prayerline: 1-800-804-3823
Orderline: 1-800-462-7426
Website: www.marian.org

Imprimi Potest:
Very Rev. Walter M. Dziordz, MIC
Provincial Superior

Stockbridge, Massachusetts
January 2002

Library of Congress Catalog Number: 2002103311

ISBN: 978-0-944203-65-1

Cover Design: Bill Sosa

For texts from the English Edition of *Diary of St. Maria Faustina Kowalska*

Nihil Obstat:
Rev. Richard Drabik, MIC
Censor

Printed in the United States of America

Mission Statement

The **Eucharistic Apostles of The Divine Mercy,** under the patronage of "the Entirely Perfect Virgin, Holy Mary" of Guadalupe, is a Roman Catholic, non-profit apostolate of the Marian Fathers of The Immaculate Conception of the B.V.M., headquartered in Stockbridge, Massachusetts, U.S.A.

Our Mission:

1) To profess and proclaim the truth of the Real Presence of Jesus in the Most Holy Eucharist, and to promote, insofar as possible, Perpetual Adoration of the Most Blessed Sacrament and the hourly offering of The Divine Mercy Chaplet for the dying;

2) To bring to a hurting world The Divine Mercy Message and Devotion according to the revelations granted to the Church through Saint Faustina Kowalska;

3) To form small faith groups, called *cenacle*s, which will meet weekly;

    a) To pray for and encourage vocations to the priesthood and the religious life;

    b) To pray and work for an end to the scourge of abortion in the world;

    c) To experience the splendor of our Catholic Faith through the study of Sacred Scripture, the *Catechism of the Catholic Church*, and the *Diary of Saint Faustina Kowalska*;

4) To encourage members in the exercise of the Faith through the spiritual and corporal works of mercy, and to help people to become sensitive to the gift and beauty of all life, especially through care for the "lepers" of today – the rejected, the lonely, the disabled, the elderly, and the dying.

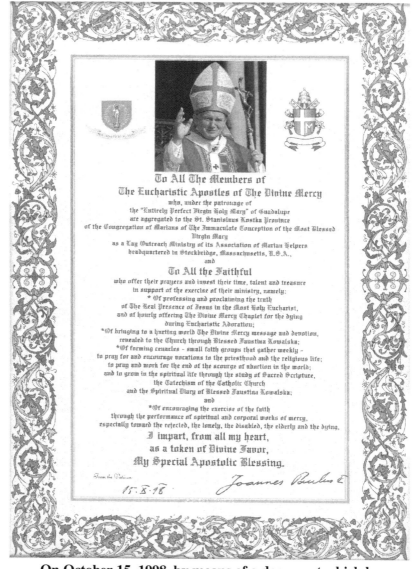

To All The Members of
The Eucharistic Apostles of The Divine Mercy
who, under the patronage of
the "Entirely Perfect Virgin Holy Mary" of Guadalupe
are aggregated to the St. Stanislaus Kostka Province
of the Congregation of Marians of The Immaculate Conception of the Most Blessed
Virgin Mary
as a Lay Outreach Ministry of its Association of Marian Helpers
headquartered in Stockbridge, Massachusetts, U.S.A.,
and

To All the Faithful
who offer their prayers and invest their time, talent and treasure
in support of the exercise of their ministry, namely:
* Of professing and proclaiming the truth
of The Real Presence of Jesus in the Most Holy Eucharist,
and of hourly offering The Divine Mercy Chaplet for the dying
during Eucharistic Adoration;
*Of bringing to a hurting world The Divine Mercy message and devotion,
revealed to the Church through Blessed Faustina Kowalska;
*Of forming cenacles - small faith groups that gather weekly -
to pray for and encourage vocations to the priesthood and the religious life;
to pray and work for the end of the scourge of abortion in the world;
and to grow in the spiritual life through the study of Sacred Scripture,
the Catechism of the Catholic Church
and the Spiritual Diary of Blessed Faustina Kowalska;
and
*Of encouraging the exercise of the faith
through the performance of spiritual and corporal works of mercy,
especially toward the rejected, the lonely, the disabled, the elderly and the dying,

I impart, from all my heart,
as a token of Divine Favor,
My Special Apostolic Blessing.

From the Vatican

15·8·98

Joannes Paulus II

On October 15, 1998, by means of a document which he
personally signed, the Holy Father, Pope John Paul II, imparted a
special Apostolic Blessing to all members of the Eucharistic
Apostles of The Divine Mercy, and to all the Faithful, who offer
their prayers and invest their time, talent and treasure in support
of the exercise of this ministry.

Dedication

The authors dedicate this book to all fellow Eucharistic Apostles around the world; all those beautiful Catholics filled with the love of God and a knowledge of His great love for mankind. May all who spread His mercy continue to be vessels and icons of mercy to a hurting world; may they continue to be the heart, hands, and feet of Jesus to those in need.

We want to especially thank our friend Dr. Robert Stackpole, Director of the John Paul II Institute of Divine Mercy, for writing sections for us on Sainthood, Heaven, Hell, and Purgatory, and for all his helpful suggestions and imput; may God reward him richly for his efforts.

CONTENTS

PART ONE SPIRITUAL READINGS

PART TWO CENACLE READING SCHEDULE

PART ONE Spiritual Readings

Praying for the Sick and Dying

An ancient Christian writer wrote, "Of all divine things, the most divine is to share with God in the saving of souls." GOD AND SOULS was the motto of St. Faustina. Our ministry's aim, as was hers, is in saving souls. Our Lord asked her to pray and offer the Chaplet for sinners and the dying, saying:

Pray as much as you can for the dying. By your entreaties [that is, insistent prayers] **obtain for them trust in My mercy, because they have most need of trust, and have it the least. Be assured that the grace of eternal salvation for certain souls in their final moment depends on your prayer. You know the whole abyss of My mercy, so draw upon it for yourself and especially for poor sinners. Sooner would heaven and earth turn into nothingness than would My mercy not embrace a trusting soul** (*Diary*, 1777).

Saint Faustina was often given the grace to know when a certain dying person desired or needed prayer; she would be alerted to the moment, by her Guardian Angel or by Our Lord Himself. At those times she would pray until she no longer felt the need to pray, or a sense of peace came upon her, or she learned that the person had died, or heard the soul say, "Thank You!" She wrote: "Oh! Dying souls are in such great need of prayer! O Jesus, inspire souls to pray often for the dying" (*Diary*, 1015).

One of the best means of assisting the dying is the one that Jesus revealed to Saint Faustina and insisted that she use often — even continuously: The Divine Mercy Chaplet. Jesus said: **My daughter, encourage souls to say the chaplet which I have given to you. It pleases Me to grant everything they ask of Me by saying the chaplet. ... Write that when they say this chaplet in the presence of the dying, I will stand between My Father and the dying person, not as the just Judge but as the merciful Savior** (*Diary*, 1541).

Earlier, Our Lord said to her, **At the hour of their death, I defend as My own glory every soul that will say this chaplet; or when others say it for a dying person, the pardon is the same** (*Diary*, 811).

What if the person prays from a distance? Saint Faustina had a love for the sick and dying, and prayed for them with great fervor. The following experiences recorded in her Diary make it clear that one does not have to be at the bedside physically. She wrote, "It sometimes happens that the dying person is in the second or third building away, yet for the spirit, space does not exist. It sometimes happens that I know about a death occurring several hundred kilometers away. This has happened several times with regard to my family and relatives and also sisters in religion, and even souls whom I have not known during their lifetime" (*Diary*, 835).

My daughter, help Me to save a certain dying sinner. Say the chaplet that I have taught you for him. When I began to say the chaplet, I saw the man dying in the midst of terrible torment and struggle. His Guardian Angel was defending him, but he was, as it were, powerless against the enormity of the soul's misery. A multitude of devils was waiting for the soul. But while I was saying the chaplet, I saw Jesus just as He is depicted in the image. The rays which issued from Jesus' Heart enveloped the sick man, and the powers of darkness fled in panic. The sick man peacefully breathed his last. When I came to myself, I understood how very important the chaplet was for the dying. It appeases the anger of God (*Diary*, 1565).

These words are particularly relevant for members of the ministry and all Eucharistic adorers. In chapels throughout the world they are reciting or praying the Chaplet for the sick and dying, and are part of an International Registry established by the ministry, and found on our Website at *www.thedivinemercy.org*.

We currently have over seventy-five Chapels worldwide praying the Divine Mercy Chaplet hourly during Eucharistic Adoration for the sick and dying. Recently fourteen cloistered convents of Poor Clares in India began participating. Moreover, on the occasion of the Great Jubilee of the year 2000, the Holy Father, Pope John Paul II, by a personally signed parchment, imparted a Special Apostolic

Blessing "to all the faithful, who during Adoration of Our Most Merciful Savior in the Most Blessed Sacrament of the altar will be praying the Divine Mercy Chaplet for the sick and for those throughout the world who will be dying in that hour." A copy of the blessing is available for Chapels whose adorers pray for the sick and dying. If interested in finding out more information on how you can obtain a copy for your Church or Chapel, please call the ministry at 1-(877)-380-0727.

Suffering

In the Morning Offering, we offer the prayers, works, and sufferings of the day in reparation for sin. All our "works" include our physical pain, mental distress, humiliations, rejections, and disappointments. Suffering can often be the result of the monotony that often represents each day, the hot summer heat, the traffic jam on the highway, or the tensions in the workplace. One form of terrible suffering is watching others suffer, especially family members or close friends. The good news is that we know our suffering can be used to help save souls. We know that offering up our suffering is possible, for St. Paul wrote, *Now I rejoice in my sufferings for your sake, and in my flesh I complete what is lacking in Christ's afflictions for the sake of His body, that is, the Church* ... (Col 1:24).

We know that Christ's Passion and His death on the Cross is a sufficient and complete sacrifice for the redemption of mankind. As followers of Christ, we make up the Mystical Body on earth, with Jesus as its Head. His "Body" still suffers in the pains and tribulations of His followers. As humans we are all sinners, and although we are forgiven of our sins after Confession, the need for reparation remains. We can offer up our sufferings for the larger Body — they have redemptive value and can build up the Body of Christ. As Eucharistic Apostles of The Divine Mercy, we ask people who are suffering to become members as "Suffering Souls," that is, those suffering, for whatever reason or cause, are asked to offer up their trials daily for the work of the ministry and the poor souls in purgatory.

The first thing that often comes to mind when speaking of suffering is the great challenge of life itself. The daily small persecutions and rejections can be as painful as a festering wound. Of course, there are many types of suffering: poor health, addictions, death of a loved one, rebellious teenagers, abusive relationships; in reality, the list is endless. Often when facing suffering or a trial of some sort, our reaction is "What did I do to deserve this?" or, "If God is so merciful, how could He let this happen?" Why does God allow the innocent to suffer, when those seen as evil seem to prosper and eat from a silver spoon? It is at these difficult times that our faith and trust in God is put to the test. The Catechism teaches us that, "Now, however, 'we walk by faith, not by sight'; we perceive God as 'in a mirror, dimly' and only 'in part.' Even though enlightened by him in whom it believes, faith is often lived in darkness and can be put to the test. The world we live in often seems very far from the one promised by faith. Our experiences of evil and suffering, injustice, and death, seem to contradict the Good News; they can shake our faith and become a temptation against it." (See *Catechism of the Catholic Church*, #164.) As followers of Christ, we know we are to be Christ-like, yet, we try to avoid all suffering. Jesus wants us to follow Him in His footsteps, telling us, *If any man would come after Me, let him deny himself and take up his cross and follow Me.* (Mt 16:24).

Sacrifice involves an element of suffering, and as St. Paul wrote, *I appeal to you therefore, brethren, by the mercies of God, to present your bodies as a living sacrifice, holy and acceptable to God* ... (Rom 12:1). Whether we like it or not, all of us will suffer during our lifetime; we live in a valley of tears. Some of us accept suffering better than others, acting like the good thief on the Cross, who used his suffering as reparation for his wrong-doings, and in return hearing these words from Jesus' lips, *Truly, I say to you, today you will be with Me in Paradise* (Lk 23:43).

Think of all the hardships we face in life, even on a daily basis: trying to pay bills, putting food on the table, and raising a family in a society that is often seen as pagan. In addition, many suffer emotional, physical, and spiritual duress, and at times all our burdens become too much to bear. Regardless of the cause or problem, pain is pain and we need to ask ourselves, what is God trying to teach me through this cross? In all walks of life, we face adversity. Our Lord told Saint Faustina, **My daughter, suffering will be a sign to you that I am with you** (*Diary*, 669). And on another occasion, He said, **My daughter, do not be afraid of sufferings; I am with you** (*Diary*, 151).

Any discussion on suffering, love, and mercy must include His Passion. Our Lord requested that we meditate on His Passion. **There is more merit to one hour of meditation on My sorrowful Passion than there is to a whole year of flagellation that draws blood; the contemplation of My painful wounds is of great prof-**

it to you, and it brings Me great joy (*Diary*, 369). **Remember My Passion, and if you do not believe My words, at least believe My wounds** (*Diary*, 379).

Saint Faustina wrote, "Today, during the Passion Service, I saw Jesus being tortured and crowned with thorns and holding a reed in His hand. Jesus was silent as the soldiers were bustling about, vying with each other in torturing Him. Jesus said nothing, but just looked at me, and in that gaze I felt His pain, so terrible that we have not the faintest idea of how much He suffered for us before He was crucified. My soul was filled with pain and longing; in my soul, I felt great hatred for sin, and even the smallest infidelity on my part seemed to me like a huge mountain for which I must expiate by mortification and penance. When I see Jesus tormented, my heart is torn to pieces, and I think: what will become of sinners if they do not take advantage of the Passion of Jesus? In His Passion, I see a whole sea of mercy" (*Diary*, 948).

Often those doing Church work find that the challenges, frustrations, and sufferings endured are so bad that they want to quit. However, let us reflect on the advice that Rev. Sopocko gave St. Faustina, "If the things you are telling me really come from God, prepare your soul for great suffering. You will encounter disapproval and persecution. They will look upon you as a hysteric and an eccentric, but the Lord will lavish His graces upon you. True works of God always meet opposition and are marked by suffering. If God wants to accomplish something, sooner or later He will do so in spite of the difficulties. Your part, in the meantime, is to arm yourself with great patience" (*Diary*, 270).

Do we accept the fact that we are imperfect, that we all have faults and weaknesses? Do we recognize that we are frail and need God as we traverse this valley of tears? Do we accept our disabilities, faults, and defects out of love for Christ? We can suffer with or without love.

Saint Faustina suffered everything with joy, patience, and perseverance. Most of us do not suffer with love, rather, we suffer out of fear, anger, anxiety, and discouragement. For many, the fear of the Cross is the greatest Cross of all. We should try to suffer out of love of God, just as Jesus suffered out of love of us. We must suffer out of love, and love while we suffer. In suffering, we share in Christ's suffering.

Our own trials of life give us an opportunity and often force us to question our relationship with God. Regarding trials, St. Faustina wrote, Strangely, God sometimes allows them, but always in order to manifest or develop virtue in our soul. That is the reason for trials. (*Diary*, 166). Suffering has a purpose, for Paul wrote, *For this slight momentary affliction is preparing us for an eternal weight of glory beyond all comparison, because we look not to the things that are seen but to the things that are unseen; for the things that are seen are transient, but the things that are unseen are eternal* (2 Cor 4:17-18). In 1 Peter 4:12-13, it is also written, *Beloved, do not be surprised at the fiery ordeal which comes upon you to prove you, as though something strange were happening to you. But rejoice insofar as you share Christ's sufferings, that you may also rejoice and be glad when His glory is revealed.*

If we allow it, suffering will open the door for spiritual growth and a realization of one's total dependence on God. For example, a person with an addiction probably will deny a problem until he hits bottom. Healing will occur through the acceptance of the problem and the realization of the need for God. When we give our sufferings and crosses back to Him, we live the words St. Paul wrote, *I have been crucified with Christ; it is no longer I who live, but Christ who lives in me; and the life I now live in the flesh I live by faith in the Son of God, who loved me and gave himself for me* (Gal 2:20). *For if we have died with Him, we will also live with Him* (2 Tim 2:11).

While Scripture is filled with accounts of healings, our particular healing will occur only if it is compatible with God's will. For those for whom suffering is part of His plan, we should reflect on Jesus' words to Saint Faustina, **Help Me, My daughter, to save souls. Join your sufferings to My Passion and offer them to the Heavenly Father for sinners** (*Diary*, 1032). And on another occasion He said, **My daughter, meditate frequently on the sufferings which I have undergone for your sake, and then nothing of what you suffer for Me will seem great to you. You please me most when you meditate on My Sorrowful Passion. Join your little sufferings to My Sorrowful Passion, so that they may have infinite value before My Majesty** (*Diary*, 1512).

We must remember that, if Jesus, as Head of the Church, suffered and was beaten and bruised on the road to Calvary, why should we as members be revered and sprayed with a sweet-smelling perfume? Our attitude of suffering should be that of Christ's. He told St. Faustina, **When I was dying on the cross, I was not thinking about Myself, but about poor sinners, and I prayed for them to My Father. I want your last moments to be completely similar to Mine on the cross. There is but one price at which souls are bought, and that is suffering united to My suffering on the cross. Pure love understands these words; carnal love will never understand them** (*Diary*, 324).

While our spirit may be strong, the flesh is weak. At times we grow weary and get discouraged. We may ask, "What good is this?" "When will it end?" or, "Why me?" but we must keep our focus on Jesus and run the good race.

What can we do with our suffering? Must it be in vain? Suffering can be a gift used for the building up of the Body of Christ, and can keep us from the hopelessness of despair. By suffering for others, we become Christ-like. *For it has been granted to you that for the sake of Christ you should not only believe in Him but also suffer for His sake, engaged in the same conflict which you saw and now hear to be mine* (Phil 1:29).

Again, St. Paul knew the value of suffering when he wrote, *Now I rejoice in my sufferings for your sake, and in my flesh I complete what is lacking in Christ's afflictions for the sake of His body, that is, the Church* (Col 1:24).

In a vision contrasting worldly people versus those who carry their cross well on earth, St. Faustina wrote, "One day, I saw two roads. One was broad, covered with sand and flowers, full of joy, music and all sorts of pleasures. People walked along it, dancing and enjoying themselves. They reached the end without realizing it. At the end of the road, there was a horrible precipice; that is, the abyss of hell. The souls fell blindly into it; as they walked, so they fell. And their number was so great it was impossible to count them. And I saw the other road, or rather, a path, for it was narrow and strewn with thorns and rocks and the people who walked along it had tears in their eyes, and all kinds of sufferings befell them. Some fell down upon the rocks, but stood up immediately and went on. At the end of the road there was a magnificent garden filled with all sorts of happiness, and all these souls entered there. At the very first instant, they forgot all their sufferings" (*Diary*, 153).

When we grow weary from the battles of daily life, let us reflect on His Passion and the reward to come to those who are faithful. Saint Faustina wrote, "There is a series of graces which God pours into the soul after these trials by fire. The soul enjoys intimate union with God. It has many visions, both corporal and intellectual. It hears many supernatural words, and sometimes distinct orders. But despite these graces, it is not self-sufficient. In fact it is even less so as a result of God's graces, because it is now open to many dangers and can easily fall prey to illusions. It ought to ask God for a spiritual director; but not only must it pray for one, it must also make every effort to find a leader who is an expert in these things, just as a military leader must know the ways along which he will lead [his followers] into battle. A soul that is united with God must be prepared for great and hard-fought battles" (*Diary*, 121).

Let us ponder the Lord's pierced heart and call upon His mercy on behalf of sinners saying, "O Blood and Water, which gushed forth from the Heart of Jesus as a fount of Mercy for us, I trust in You" (*Diary*, 187).

To Be a Saint

What is a "saint"?

There is a story told about a priest who asked this question of his congregation one Sunday morning. He told them that a saint is not necessarily someone famous or influential in worldly terms, but someone who practices virtue to a heroic degree. While he was speaking, however a little girl was sitting in the pews, gazing at the saints in the stained-glass windows of the Church. Suddenly, she jumped up on the pew and called out: "I know! A saint is someone who lets the light shine through!"

Perhaps there is no better description of a saint than someone so completely surrendered to God's truth, God's will, and God's grace that he/she becomes utterly transparent to the "light" of His merciful love. Saint Faustina wrote: "Today during meditation, God gave me inner light and understanding as to what sanctity is and of what it consists ... Neither graces, nor revelations, nor raptures, nor gifts granted to a soul make it perfect, but rather the intimate union of the soul with God. ... My sanctity and perfection consists in the close union of my will with the will of God" (*Diary*, 1107).

And on another occasion, "My Jesus, penetrate me through and through so that I might be able to reflect You in my whole life. Divinize me so that my deeds may have supernatural value. Grant that I may have love, compassion, and mercy for every soul without exception. O my Jesus, each of Your saints reflects one of Your virtues; I desire to reflect Your compassionate heart, full of mercy; I want to glorify it. Let Your mercy, O Jesus, be impressed upon my heart and soul like a seal, and this will be my badge in this and the future life. Glorifying your mercy is the exclusive task of my life" (*Diary*, 1242).

Saint Faustina teaches us not only the meaning of sanctity, but tells us the three most important dispositions that we must have if we are to attain it.

To begin with, we need to have a fervent *desire* to become saints, as the first desire of our hearts. Saint Faustina wrote, "My Jesus, You know that from my earliest years I have wanted to become a great saint; that is to say, I have wanted to love You with a love so great that there would be no soul who has hitherto loved You so. At first these desires of mine were kept secret, and only Jesus knew of them. But today I cannot contain them within my heart; I would like to cry out to the whole world, 'Love God, because He is good and great is His mercy!' " (*Diary*, 1372).

The second thing we need to have is great trust in Jesus, for His mercy is so much greater than our sins and miseries. "In spite of my wretchedness, I want to become a saint, and I trust that God's mercy can make a saint even out of such misery as I am" (*Diary*, 1333). Jesus told her, **The greatest sinners would achieve great sanctity, if only they would trust in My mercy** (*Diary*, 1784). And on another occasion, **When a soul approaches Me with trust, I fill it with such an abundance of graces that it cannot contain them within itself, but radiates them to other souls** (*Diary*, 1074).

Finally, our journey toward sanctity is not something we have to do on our own. We are surrounded by "a great cloud of witnesses" (Heb 12:1) who assist us by their prayers and heavenly friendship. "They do not cease to intercede with the Father for us, as they proffer the merits which they acquired on earth through the one mediator between God and Men, Christ Jesus. ... So by their fraternal concern is our weakness greatly helped" (*Lumen Gentium*, 49).

Saint Faustina promised to come to our aid, writing, "I feel certain that my mission will not come to an end upon my death, but will begin. O doubting souls, I will draw aside for you the veils of heaven to convince you of God's goodness, so that you will no longer continue to wound with your distrust the sweetest Heart of Jesus. God is Love and Mercy" (*Diary*, 281).

As saints under construction, let us never waiver in our hope and desire of achieving great sanctity, picking ourselves up after we fall, and continually trying to run the good race.

Eucharist — The Bread of Life

Any discussion on The Divine Mercy must include the Eucharist, as they are one and the same. That is to say, The Divine Mercy Incarnate *is* Jesus, and Jesus *is* the Eucharist.

Just as blood carries life-sustaining oxygen and nutrients to all the cells in our body, the Eucharist is our spiritual food and transfuses us with life-saving grace and power of the Holy Spirit. Jesus is the sacrificial lamb, who gave of His life out of love for us. *But I was like a gentle lamb led to the slaughter* (Jer 11:19). *You know that you were ransomed from the futile ways inherited from your ancestors, not with perishable things like silver or gold, but with the precious blood of Christ, like that of a lamb without defect or blemish* (1 Pet 1:18-19). The Eucharist is food for our spiritual journey, and provides us nourishment and grace for our travels on the road of life.

On Holy Thursday, Jesus instituted the Most Blessed Sacrament, the Eucharist, and the gift is ongoing and celebrated daily in Masses all over the world. He wants us to partake in this gift as frequently as our station in life permits. *Very truly, I tell you, unless you eat the flesh of the Son of Man and drink His blood, you have no life in you. Those who eat My flesh and drink My blood have eternal life, and I will raise them up on the last day* (Jn 6:53-54).

The Church teaches that at the moment of Consecration during the Mass, the bread and wine on the altar become the Body and Blood of Jesus Christ. To reaffirm Catholic teaching, and in response to the catechisms being published by Luther and others during the Protestant Reformation, the Council of Trent in 1551 condemned the opinion that Christ is present only in the elements as in a sign, or that Christ is received only spiritually. *I am the bread of life. Your ancestors ate manna in the wilderness, and they died. This is the bread that comes down from heaven, so that one may eat of it and not die. I am the living bread that came down from heaven. Whoever eats of this bread will live forever; and the bread that I will give for the life of the world is My flesh* (Jn 6:48-51). After the Consecration, the bread and wine cease to exist although the appearance and natural properties remain; this change is called transubstantiation. While it is true that God is everywhere spiritually, the Eucharistic presence of Christ, that is, that Christ is present Body, Blood, Soul and Divinity is called the True Presence, or the Real Presence.

When discussing the Real Presence, one can see from the 6th Chapter of John that even at the time of Christ there was much disagreement and discussion and many did not understand what He was saying. In John 6:48-56, He speaks about being the living bread which came down from Heaven, and that anyone who eats of this bread will live forever. And he added, *for My flesh is true food and My blood is true drink*. However, in verse 60, it is written that many of His disciples, when they heard it, said, *This teaching is difficult; who can accept it?* And in verse 66 it is written, *Because of this many of his disciples turned back and no longer went about with Him*. But Our Lord did not change it — even if it meant losing His twelve Apostles. For, He turned to them and said "Do you also want to leave?" On behalf of the group, Peter replied with complete love and devotion, "To whom shall we go? You have the words of eternal life. We have believed and have come to know that You are the Holy One of God." From that point the Eucharist was a sharp dividing line between those who believed and those who didn't. The early Christians who believed suffered much due to persecution, and there were many martyrs. People met and prayed in secret, and could not openly discuss their faith. As a result, a community of secrecy developed as reflected in the signs and symbols of the early Church, ones that could not be deciphered by pagans due to their complexity.

When the catacombs were discovered and excavated, several symbols were found in far greater frequency than others. They reflected on the meaning of life and the "Great Secret" — the Real Presence of Jesus Christ in the Eucharist. Interestingly, it was not Christ's Resurrection, His numerous healings, the Sermon on the Mount, or the Passion that predominated in the symbolic artwork of the catacombs. Rather, it was the symbol of the Eucharist that was the focus throughout the catacombs, and even on Peter's tomb.

Saint Faustina realized the great gift of the Eucharist and added to her name, Sister Maria Faustina *"of the Blessed Sacrament."* She wrote, "If the angels were capable of envy, they would envy us for two things; one is the receiving of Holy Communion, and the other is suffering" (*Diary*, 1804). Our Lord wants us to receive Him in Holy Communion frequently and visit Him in the Blessed Sacrament. He desires to lavish graces on us, but many remain indifferent. **They treat Me as a dead object, whereas My Heart is full of love and mercy. In order that you may know of at least some of My pain, imagine the most tender of mothers who has great love for her children, while those children spurn her love. Consider her pain. No one is in a position to console her. This is but a feeble image and likeness of My love** (*Diary*, 1447).

The power of the Sacrament is that it restores us to God's grace and allows us to join with Him in an ongoing intimate relationship. The Sacrament may provide much peace and contentment to the sinner who shows remorse and a contrite heart for his venial sins. The Church teaches that the communicant must receive in a state of grace, and mortal sins must be confessed prior to receiving the Eucharist. *Whoever, therefore, eats the bread or drinks the cup of the Lord in an unworthy manner will be answerable for the body and blood of the Lord* (1 Cor 11:27). As we are all part of the mystical body of the church, the Sacrament also reconciles us with the Church and works to revitalize it from the injury of one of its members.

Not only are we to receive the Eucharist, we must also live the Eucharist. We are to let Jesus enter into every cell of our body and be expressions of His great love. We are to be icons of Mercy, radiating Love and Mercy out to others.

You are the light of the world. A city built on a hill cannot be hid. No one after lighting a lamp puts it under the bushel basket, but on the lampstand, and it gives light to all in the house. In the same way, let your light shine before others, so that they may see your good works and give glory to your Father in heaven (Mt 5:14-16).

Heaven

The New Testament tells us many times of the eternal joy that awaits the friends of God. Saint Paul wrote: *I consider that the sufferings of this present time are not worth comparing with the glory that is to be revealed to us* (Rom 8:18). *For this slight momentary affliction is preparing for us an eternal weight of glory beyond all comparison* (2 Cor 4:17-18). He wrote in Colossians, *No eye has seen, nor ear heard, nor the heart of man conceived what God has prepared for those who love Him* (Col 2:9).

Saint Faustina also found it almost impossible to describe the joys of heaven that she saw in a vision, "Today I was in heaven, in spirit, and I saw its inconceivable beauties and the happiness that awaits us after death. I saw how all creatures give ceaseless praise and glory to God. I saw how great is happiness in God, which spreads to all creatures, making them happy; and then all the glory and praise which springs from this happiness returns to its source; and they enter into the depths of God, contemplating the inner life of God — the Father, the Son, and the Holy Spirit, whom they will never understand or fathom" (*Diary*, 777).

For St. Faustina, to be in heaven is to be immersed in God, in the ocean of His mercy, and embraced by His love forever. "O Lord, immerse my soul in the ocean of Your divinity, and grant me the grace of knowing You; for the better I know You, the more I desire You, and the more my love for you grows. I feel in my soul an unfathomable abyss which only God can fill. I lose myself in Him as a drop does in the ocean" (*Diary*, 605). And, "the more I come to know the greatness of God, the more joyful I become that He is as He is. And I rejoice immensely in His greatness and am delighted that I am so little because, since I am so little, He carries me in His arms and holds me close to His Heart" (*Diary*, 779).

Above all, to be in heaven is to be forever with Jesus, for He promised: *And when I go and prepare a place for you, I will come again and will take you to myself, that where I am you may be also* (Jn 14:2-3). As the *Catechism of the Catholic Church* states, "Those who die in God's grace and friendship and are perfectly purified live forever with Christ. They are like God forever, for they see Him as He is, face to face" (*Catechism*, #1023-1024).

This perfect life with the Most Holy Trinity — this communion of life and love with the Trinity, with the Virgin Mary, the angels and all the blessed — is called "heaven." Heaven is the ultimate end and fulfillment of the deepest human longings, the state of supreme, definitive happiness.

Hell

Saint Faustina writes in her *Diary*, entry #741, of a vision she once had of the terrors of hell. Yet we need to interpret this frightening vision in the context of the rest of her diary. In entry 1588, for example, our Lord told her that He metes out punishment to impenitent souls only with great reluctance, **I do not want to punish mankind, but I desire to heal it, pressing it to my Merciful Heart. I use punishment when they force me to do so; My hand is reluctant to take hold of the sword of justice** (*Diary*, 1588).

On another occasion, St. Faustina states that the ultimate punishment — eternal damnation — is essentially a self-chosen state: "I received a deeper understanding of divine mercy. Only that soul who wants it [damnation] will be damned, for God condemns no one" (*Diary*, 1452). This fits perfectly with the *Catechism* definition of "hell" as a "state of definitive self-exclusion from communion with God" (*Catechism*, #1033).

Remember that to deliberately throw away communion with God, the source of all good, is to lose *everything*. The "torments" of hell described by St. Faustina, therefore — loss of God, remorse with no hope of change, fire that penetrates but does not destroy, despair, darkness, stench, the company of Satan, hatred of God, vile words, curses, blasphemies, torments of the senses — all of this is probably a fairly accurate description of what total eternal loss would be like, both spiritually and physically. And this sobering truth is related in the words of Christ in the gospels, and in the *Catechism* (1034-1036).

Saint Faustina does not actually say that *God* is the one who "tortures" the soul in hell, or that He is the one who "designed" special torments for each particular kind of sinner. Catholic tradition has it — through the visions of other saints — that it is Satan and his demons who do that. After all, to reject God is to choose instead the everlasting company of those who reject Him! And yet, in another sense, it is true that this state of irrevocable "self-exclusion" from God, the source of all good, with all its inevitable self-destructive effects, is something that in His justice,

God permits. As St. Thomas Aquinas would say, it is God's "consequent will," not His "absolute will."

At one point, St. Faustina says that she saw a "fire that will penetrate the soul without destroying it — a terrible suffering, since it is a purely spiritual fire, lit by God's anger" (*Diary*, 741). God's anger is not an emotion, nor vindictiveness, but His total, unrelenting, active opposition to evil. What burns the soul in a "spiritual" way, we may surmise, is to be unavoidably confronted with the full truth about one's evil deeds and irreversible rejection of God's love, and to hear Christ Jesus Himself ratify that truth with the words, *Depart from Me, you cursed, into the eternal fire prepared for the devil and his angels* (Mt 25:41). In the end, "the truth will win out," and God will not be mocked.

Yet, God is so merciful that He has even assumed our human condition, dying on the Cross for us, in order to save us from such an eternal loss. Saint Faustina's teaching about hell, therefore, magnifies God's mercy, for it shows us clearly the greatest evil from which God wants to rescue us.

In fact, as many of the saints teach, even hell itself is tempered by God's mercy (e.g. St. Catherine of Siena, St. John Eudes). By allowing souls to reject Him and His love forever, God thereby respects human freedom — the ability He gave us to choose our own destiny.

Moreover, God knows that for souls who truly hate Him, to see Him face to face forever would make them even more miserable than their self-chosen exile. That is why Cardinal Newman wrote: "heaven would be hell to the irreligious" — and Milton's Satan in *Paradise Lost* voices the sentiments of all damned: "Better to reign in hell than serve in heaven." As C.S. Lewis put it: "The gates of hell are locked from the *inside*."

Purgatory

The Church's teaching on purgatory is summarized in the *Catechism of The Catholic Church*, paragraph 1030:

"All who die in God's grace and friendship, but still imperfectly purified, are indeed assured of their eternal salvation; but after death they undergo purification, so as to achieve the holiness necessary to enter the joy of heaven."

Elaborating further on the teaching of Church Tradition on this matter, Fr. Kenneth Baker, S.J., wrote in *Fundamentals of Catholicism* (vol. 3), "The souls in purgatory, after their particular judgement, know for certain that they are saved; in this they rejoice. But since they need cleansing, they are separated from God for a time. This separation is most painful to them, since their whole being longs to be united with God."

Clearly, this "purifying" and "cleansing" of souls in purgatory is an expression of the Mercy of God, and not merely of His Justice. On the one hand, it is only just that those who were partially and imperfectly penitent for their sins on earth should make up their debt to divine justice by undergoing "purgatorial or cleansing punishments" after their death (Council of Lyons, 1274). On the other hand, this divine punishment is more remedial than retributive. In other words, God intends it for the healing and rehabilitation of the soul. Much as a person might need to have a tooth pulled in order to restore his dental health, so the soul can only attain full health by the uprooting of its inordinate attachment to creatures, and especially its own pride and ego. This healing process for the soul is painful, but necessary if the soul is ever to be prepared for heaven, and attain *the holiness without which no one will see the Lord* (Heb 12:14). Thus, God purifies imperfect souls by punishing them in a way that heals them, making them holy, and ready for heavenly joy. In this way, the Lord's Justice is exercised with great Mercy.

The Church has never precisely defined the pains of purgatory. But some of the saints have reasoned that it consists primarily in the spiritual pain of "longing for God," and several saints have had private revelations to that effect as well (e.g., St. Catherine of Genoa). Saint Alphonsus Liguori wrote that for the souls in purgatory, "the supernatural love of God with which they burn draws them with such violence to be united to [God], that when they see the barrier which their sins have put in the way, they feel a pain so acute that if they were capable of death, they could not live a moment" (*The Great Means of Salvation*, no. 20).

Nevertheless, the saints do not teach us about the sufferings of the souls in purgatory primarily in order to frighten us, but in order to move us with compassion to come to their aid. As St. Augustine wrote: "One of the holiest works, one of the best exercises of piety that we can practice in this world, is to offer sacrifices, alms, and prayers for the dead" (Homily 16). To pray for the souls in purgatory is truly a work of mercy.

Look up some of the Scripture passages in which the doctrine of purgatory has its roots: 2 Mac 12:42-46; Mt 5:25-26; 12:32; 1 Cor 3:11-15; Heb 12:14. After reading them, you will see that the doctrine is more implicit in these passages than explicit. These implications were drawn out and clarified in the ancient and medieval eras by the saints, doctors, and Magisterium of the Church. The teachings of the Church and of the saints were confirmed and vividly expressed in a vision of purgatory received by St. Faustina, as she recorded in her *Diary*. It is a summary of the Catholic understanding of purgatory:

> [The next night] I saw my Guardian Angel, who ordered me to follow him. In a moment I was in a misty place full of fire in which there was a great crowd of suffering souls. They were praying fervently, but to no avail, for themselves; only we can come to their aid. The flames which were burning them did not touch me at all. My Guardian Angel did not leave me for an instant. I asked these souls what their greatest suffering was. They answered me in one voice that their greatest torment was longing for God. I saw our Lady visiting the souls in purgatory. The souls call her 'The Star of the Sea.' She brings them refreshment...We went out of that prison of suffering. [I heard an interior voice] which said, **My mercy does not want this, but justice demands it.** Since that time, I am in closer communion with the suffering souls (*Diary*, 20).

Reflecting on his departed wife, C.S. Lewis wrote in *A Grief Observed*, "She was a splendid thing; a soul straight, bright, and tempered like a sword. But not a perfect saint. A sinful woman married to a sinful man; two of God's patients, not yet cured. I know there are not only tears to be dried but stains to be scoured. The sword will be made even brighter. ... But oh God, tenderly, tenderly."

One of the charisms of the Marian Fathers of the Immaculate Conception is to pray for the poor souls in purgatory. Let us never forget these souls; let us pray for them, and ask them to pray for us when they reach their final reward in Heaven.

WEEKLY CENACLE
READING SCHEDULE

WEEK 101 — *Diary*, 942-951

ADDITIONAL READING ASSIGNMENT TO PREPARE FOR THIS WEEK:

Scripture - Lam 1:16; Prov 3:5; Rom 4:18; 2 Cor 5:7;
Ps 25:1-2

Catechism - #164

WEEKLY OVERVIEW:

The feeling of desolation in Sister's soul and mistrust of herself, as well as her closeness with God, are reviewed. Prayerful reading of *Diary* entry #949 is recommended.

LEARNING AND DISCUSSION:

Describe recent situations where you felt desolation in your soul, and have better appreciated your own weaknesses and wretchedness. What did Saint Faustina rely on in times of desolation? (*Diary*, 944)

1) Is familiarity with God a detriment to His honor and Majesty? (*Diary*, 947)

2) Saint Faustina wrote, "In His Passion, I see a whole sea of mercy" (*Diary,* 948). Give examples of how God's mercy is evident amidst our own trials and sufferings, especially in the family and workplace. (*Catechism*, #164).

3) Discuss "The love of God is the flower — mercy the fruit," and how we are to apply this to daily situations. Reflect on a situation at work where this statement applied.

LESSON GOALS:

At the end of the discussion, members should understand:

- A better understanding that a deeper realization of our weaknesses is important for growth as we become more dependent on God's mercy.
- Closeness and familiarity to God is not a detriment to His honor and majesty.
- Mercy is the fruit of our love of neighbor.

WEEK 102 — Read the article "Praying for the Sick and Dying"

WEEKLY OVERVIEW:

The readings discuss the promises associated with recitation of the Divine Mercy Chaplet, as well as the efforts of the ministry in getting the Chaplet recited in Adoration Chapels worldwide for the intention of the sick and dying.

LEARNING AND DISCUSSION:

1) What was the motto of St. Faustina?
2) What are the promises associated with recitation of the Chaplet? How can members spread recitation of the Chaplet to those in nursing homes, hospitals, prisons, etc.?
3) What did the Lord promise to those who recite the Chaplet?

LESSON GOALS:

At the end of the discussion, members should understand:

- A better understanding of the promises associated with recitation of The Divine Mercy Chaplet, as well as the effort of the ministry to spread recitation during Eucharistic Adoration.

WEEK 103 — Read the article "To Be a Saint."

ADDITIONAL READING ASSIGNMENT TO PREPARE FOR THIS WEEK:

Scripture - Mt 5:48

Catechism - #2013-15, 2031

WEEKLY OVERVIEW:

The desire to become a saint and the path of holiness are topics of discussion. Also, St. Faustina's writings on the three dispositions necessary to become a saint are discussed.

LEARNING AND DISCUSSION:

1) Is becoming a saint one of our priorities? Do we share this desire with others?
2) What are three dispositions necessary to become a saint?
3) How is the way of perfection related to the Way of the Cross? Can you relate to this in your daily life?

LESSON GOALS:
At the end of the discussion, members should understand:
- How we are all called to be saints.
- Saints had a fervent desire to become saints and "ran the good race."

WEEK 104 — *Diary*, 952-968

ADDITIONAL READING ASSIGNMENT TO PREPARE FOR THIS WEEK:
Scripture - Job 1:8-12; 13:12; 42:10-17
Catechism - #606-607

WEEKLY OVERVIEW:
The readings for the week focus on suffering, submission, the saving of souls, and living in His divine will.

LEARNING AND DISCUSSION:
1) How can suffering, which is often erroneously perceived as punishment from God, be used for the honor and glory of God? (*Diary*, 953)
2) Does God reward for successful outcomes, or for the labor and good will undertaken? (*Diary*, 952)
   Give practical examples where this is relevant.
3) Can the offering of mundane sufferings assist in the conversion of souls? (*Diary*, 961)
4) What is more important than sacrifice in living our lives? (*Diary*, 955)

LESSON GOALS:
At the end of the discussion, members should understand:
- The meaning of suffering in the Christian context, especially in conversion and the saving of souls.
- The importance of trying to live in accord with God's will.
- God rewards for the effort, and not the results.

WEEK 105 — *Diary*, 968-992

ADDITIONAL READING ASSIGNMENT TO PREPARE FOR THIS WEEK:
Scripture - Deut 6:4-5; Mt 22:35-40
Catechism - #2633, 2643, 1822, 1826

WEEKLY OVERVIEW:
The readings discuss St. Faustina's deep mystical union

with God, as well as Our Lord's request to continually pray for the dying. She writes that the "greatest greatness is to love God." She feels like a royal child as the blood of Jesus is circulating in her veins.

LEARNING AND DISCUSSION:

1) Why do we recite the Divine Mercy Chaplet for the intentions of the sick and dying? How can this be spread in your area so those visiting nursing homes and hospitals can be made aware (*Diary*, 975 and 1541)

2) Think of examples where you did a good deed but it was not done out of love. What is true greatness? (*Diary*, 990)

3) Many souls are afraid to approach God as they fear Him, especially the dying. What does Our Lord ask her to do with regards to these souls? (*Diary*, 975, 1777)

4) Discuss St. Faustina's comment about the Blood of Jesus circulating in her veins, and our reception of the Eucharist (*Diary*, 992).

LESSON GOALS:

At the end of the discussion, members should understand:

- The need to pray for the dying.
- How after Holy Communion we too are like royal children, having the Blood of Jesus in our veins.
- Love must be the drawing force of all our actions.

WEEK 106 — Read the article "Eucharist—The Bread of Life"

ADDITIONAL READING ASSIGNMENT TO PREPARE FOR THIS WEEK:

Scripture - Jn 6
Catechism - #1377, 1381

WEEKLY OVERVIEW:

The readings discuss the great gift of the Eucharist, St. Faustina's love for the Eucharist, and how we are to live the love of Jesus in our lives.

LEARNING AND DISCUSSION:

1) How is the Eucharist our spiritual food?

2) How do the rays in the Image represent the Sacraments of Mercy?

3) What title did St. Faustina add to her name?

LESSON GOALS:

At the end of the discussion, members should understand:

- The great gift of the Eucharist.
- How we are to receive the Eucharist, and then live the Eucharistic love of Jesus.

WEEK 107 — *Diary*, 993-1002

ADDITIONAL READING ASSIGNMENT TO PREPARE FOR THIS WEEK:

Scripture - Jn 13:34; 1 Cor 3:16; Mt 22:35-40; Gal 5:22

Catechism - #164-5, 1508

WEEKLY OVERVIEW:

The readings emphasize the beauty and value of suffering, and how God's love sweetened St. Faustina's fate. God's command for her to do all she can for the work of mercy is noteworthy.

LEARNING AND DISCUSSION:

1) St. Faustina writes that it is no great thing to love God in prosperity. How can we apply this to our own lives, reflecting on how we act in times of prosperity versus adversity?

2) Sister writes in *Diary* entry #997, "Happy the soul that knows how to love unreservedly." Discuss how our love is often conditional, especially to those whom we love most.

3) What gives strength to the humble soul? (*Diary*, 1000) Give examples of how we can take advantage of this in daily life.

LESSON GOALS:

At the end of the discussion, members should understand:

- The need for unconditional love of oneself and others.
- How suffering can draw us nearer to God, that the strength of souls comes from the fount of mercy, and that we are called to be vessels of mercy to a hurting world.

WEEK 108 — *Diary*, 1003-1025

ADDITIONAL READING ASSIGNMENT TO PREPARE FOR THIS WEEK:
Scripture - Mt 27:26-35; Rom 5:1; Col 3:12-15; Mt 5:16
Catechism - #1829, 1832, 2299, 2305, 2447

WEEKLY OVERVIEW:

The readings focus on the work of imploring mercy for the whole world, prayer for the dying, and the inner peace St. Faustina had in spite of adversity.

LEARNING AND DISCUSSION:

1) St. Faustina experienced the Passion (#1010) in her own body. In what ways do we experience the Passion in our daily lives?

2) Sister had a strong urging in her soul to "begin the work" (#1013). In what ways can we continue this work, in our family, cenacle group, and local parish?

3) In *Diary* entry #1022, St. Faustina mentions her interior life and interior silence. She speaks of many sufferings and adversities. What trials did you encounter since our last meeting, and how did you maintain inner peace?

LESSON GOALS:

At the end of the discussion, members should understand:

• The struggle to maintain an inner peace, in spite of adversity and trial.

• The urgent call to spread the message of mercy and continue St. Faustina's call to be an apostle of mercy.

• Our struggles are an opportunity to share in His Passion.

WEEK 109 — *Diary*, 1026-1046

ADDITIONAL READING ASSIGNMENT TO PREPARE FOR THIS WEEK:
Scripture - Mt 25:31-46; Jn 19:28; Jn 6:49-51
Catechism - #1038-41, 1680-82, 1689

WEEKLY OVERVIEW:

The readings discuss a variety of topics rich in spirituality. Saint Faustina writes of Jesus' thirst for souls, her realization of the need to pray for dying souls, reflections on how Holy Communion sustains her, a vision of Rome and Poland on the Feast Day, and how amidst terrible torments her understanding that the sun is not extinguished.

LEARNING AND DISCUSSION:

1) What works of mercy can we do in the home or workplace that we often neglect or overlook?
2) Why is it important to pray for dying souls? (*Diary*, 1797) Do we have a thirst for saving souls?
3) St. Faustina is confident during times of terrible torment because she understood that "the Sun is not extinguished." How can we apply this to our own lives?
4) The Feast of Divine Mercy is mentioned in the readings. Discuss the promises of the Feast Day (*Diary*, 300 and 742) as well as *Diary* entry #180, paragraph three. Compare and contrast the Merciful God with the perception many people have of a cruel and punishing God.

LESSON GOALS:

At the end of the discussion, members should understand:

- The Communion of Saints and the need to pray for dying souls
- The need for trust in times of trial
- The many opportunities placed before us daily to do spiritual and corporal works of mercy

WEEK 110 — Read the article on "Suffering"

ADDITIONAL READING ASSIGNMENT TO PREPARE FOR THIS WEEK:

Scripture - Mt 16:24; 2 Cor 4:17-18; Col 1:24
Catechism - #164

WEEKLY OVERVIEW:

We are all called to be Christ-like. This involves suffering as we traverse the earth as pilgrims on a journey. The role of redemptive suffering in life is the main theme.

LEARNING AND DISCUSSION:

1) What are ways in which we suffer?
2) What did Father Sopocko tell St. Faustina about suffering? (*Diary*, 270)

3) How does the message of mercy convey hope?
(*Diary*, 153)

LESSON GOALS:

At the end of the discussion, members should understand:
- The role of redemptive suffering in our lives.
- How we are called to suffer in our journey on earth.

WEEK 111 — *Diary*, 1047-1062

ADDITIONAL READING ASSIGNMENT TO PREPARE FOR THIS WEEK:

Scripture - Ezek 36:26
Catechism - #1451

WEEKLY OVERVIEW:

St. Faustina speaks on suffering, the devil's traps and snares set for souls of priests, and the Novena before the Feast Day.

LEARNING AND DISCUSSION:

1) In *Diary* entry #1052, St. Faustina writes of hardened hearts being converted. How is the message of Divine Mercy a "heart" message and not a "head" message?
2) Sister wrote in *Diary* entry #1054 that she would not have exchanged martyrdom for all the pleasures in the world. How can suffering bring us closer to God?
3) In *Diary* entry #1059, she was commanded to begin a novena for the conversion of the whole world. Give examples and discuss in what ways the world needs conversion, especially those you encounter daily?
4) Should the greatest sinner have fear in approaching Jesus? (*Diary*, 1059)

LESSON GOALS:

At the end of the discussion, members should understand:
- That God's mercy is greater than our worst sin.
- The message of Divine Mercy calls us to conversion of the heart.
- How trials can bring us closer to God.

Week 112 — *Diary*, 1063-1084
Additional Reading Assignment to Prepare For This Week:
Scripture - Mt 5:7; Mt 5:14-16
Catechism - #1378, 1418
Weekly Overview:
The readings discuss trials, Eucharistic Adoration, and spreading of the devotion to the Divine Mercy.
Learning and Discussion:
1) What is St. Faustina's strength in times of difficulty? (*Diary*, 1065) Why did she pray for a guard upon her lips?
2) Why did the Lord ask St. Faustina to tell the superior to establish Eucharistic Adoration? (*Diary*, 1050)
3) What did the Lord promise to souls who spread the honor of His mercy? (*Diary*, 1075)
Lesson Goals:
At the end of the discussion, members should understand:
- The importance of reliance and dependence on God in all situations.
- The need for Eucharistic Adoration to implore God's mercy.
- The promise made for those who spread the honor of God's mercy.

Week 113 — *Diary*, 1085-1104
Additional Reading Assignment to Prepare For This Week:
Scripture - Mt 6:30-34; Rom 3:23-25; Rom 11:32
Catechism - #2088
Weekly Overview:
Temptation & discouragement, doing God's will, and divine illuminations are topics covered in the readings.
Learning and Discussion:
1) St. Faustina speaks of temptation followed by discouragement (*Diary*, 1086). What are the greatest obstacles to holiness? (*Diary*, 1488) How do we let discouragement and anxiety become obstacles to holiness?
2) If the Lord demands something of a soul, He gives it the means to carry it out, and through grace, makes it

capable of doing this. Do you let those suffering around you understand this? What is grace? (*Catechism* #2003-2004)

3) St. Faustina speaks about times in her life of spiritual insight and divine illumination; these are times of great inner knowledge which God imparts to the soul. Reflect on times in your life where God imparted such knowledge.

LESSON GOALS:

At the end of the discussion, members should understand:

- The pitfall and trap of temptation and discouragement.
- The importance of doing God's will.
- Divine illumination in our lives.

WEEK 114 — *Diary*, 1105-1122

ADDITIONAL READING ASSIGNMENT TO PREPARE FOR THIS WEEK:

Scripture - Mt 19:30; Mt 23-12; Luke 1:47-48
Catechism - #1805-1806

WEEKLY OVERVIEW:

The cardinal virtue of prudence, humility and Saint Faustina's internal sufferings are topics discussed.

LEARNING AND DISCUSSION:

1) St. Faustina speaks of prudence, and how virtue without prudence is not virtue at all. What is prudence? (*Catechism* #1806)

2) St. Faustina said that the sufferings of martyrs were not as great as her internal sufferings. Do your internal daily sufferings, or those you encounter, at times seem so great that you wonder how you can handle the burden?

3) Sister speaks of humility. How is Our Lady the role model of humility?

LESSON GOALS:

At the end of the discussion, members should understand:

- The cardinal virtue of prudence, internal sufferings, trials and humility.

WEEK 115 — Read the article on "Heaven"

ADDITIONAL READING ASSIGNMENT TO PREPARE FOR THIS WEEK:
>Scripture - Rev 21:3-5
>
>Catechism - #325-326, 1023-1029

WEEKLY OVERVIEW:
>The concept of the splendor and grandeur of heaven is the theme for the week.

LEARNING AND DISCUSSION:
>1) According to the Scriptural passages in the article, as well as Rev 21:25, discuss the promises of Scripture regarding the heavenly kingdom.
>2) How would we face the sufferings of life differently — even death itself — if we truly believed in heaven?
>3) According to the *Catechism* and the writings of St. Faustina, is it possible to find your heart's desire? Where can it be found?

LESSON GOALS:
>At the end of the discussion, members should understand:
>- The splendor of heaven.
>- The great cloud of witnesses who intercede for us.

WEEK 116 — *Diary*, 1123-1147

ADDITIONAL READING ASSIGNMENT TO PREPARE FOR THIS WEEK:
>Scripture - Lk 6:27-31; Lk 18:10-14
>
>Catechism - #1765, 1825, 1849

WEEKLY OVERVIEW:
>The need for love, knowledge of God, self-love, and the need to see all things in a spiritual context are topics for discussion.

LEARNING AND DISCUSSION:
>1) Saint Faustina wrote, "Only love is able to cross over precipices and mountain peaks." Discuss situations in our lives where anger and resentment took away our inner peace and kept us at the base of the mountain.
>2) Why is it necessary to frequently assess our motives and act accordingly? (*Diary,* 1139)
>3) In *Diary* entry #1141, she speaks of the soul with only one foot on the ground. What does she mean? What

are ways in which we let the concerns of the world keep both feet on the ground?

4) Does the merciful Savior punish the sinner that asks for graces and returns to Him in sorrow? (*Diary*, 1146)

LESSON GOALS:

At the end of the discussion, members should understand:

- How important love is in allowing us to cross the mountains of life.
- The importance of keeping our eyes focused on the spiritual world.
- The depth of God's mercy and having an appreciation for that mercy.
- The need for trust in His mercy.

WEEK 117 — *Diary*, 1148-1165

ADDITIONAL READING ASSIGNMENT TO PREPARE FOR THIS WEEK:

Scripture - Sir 28:13-16; Tit 3:2-4

Catechism - #2477, 2479, 2507

WEEKLY OVERVIEW:

The importance of using our tongue to speak kind words and avoiding slander is discussed, as well as ways of being merciful.

LEARNING AND DISCUSSION:

1) St. Faustina writes of how a lay person spoke fictitious things about her and, as a result, her heart felt a twinge of pain. In what ways do we slander, gossip, and hurt people with our words.

2) She wrote that when pain overwhelmed her soul, her strength was Jesus crucified. What ways do we often turn to alternatives to handle our pain and suffering?

3) Discuss the three aspects of His will in *Diary* entry #1155, and how we are part of this plan. What are the three ways of performing an act of mercy? Give examples where we can do this at work and at home.

LESSON GOALS:

At the end of the discussion, members should understand:

- How important it is that our tongue be used to speak only good of others.

- Jesus is our strength in times of suffering.
- That Eucharistic Apostles must continue to pray, perform spiritual and corporal works of mercy, and evangelize others in the Faith.

WEEK 118 — Read the article on "HELL"

ADDITIONAL READING ASSIGNMENT TO PREPARE FOR THIS WEEK:
Catechism - #633, 1034-1037

WEEKLY OVERVIEW:
The existence of Hell and St. Faustina's description of Hell are discussed in this lesson.

LEARNING AND DISCUSSION:
1) Is Jesus eager to banish souls to Hell for all eternity? What did he say to St. Faustina about this?
2) Does God cast souls into Hell against their will? Explain and discuss.
3) If God allows souls to reject His love forever, choosing damnation instead, how does this show us Divine Mercy?

LESSON GOALS:
At the end of the discussion, members should understand:
- The existence of Hell.
- We send ourselves to Hell.

WEEK 119 — *Diary*, 1166-1188

ADDITIONAL READING ASSIGNMENT TO PREPARE FOR THIS WEEK:
Scripture - Gen 17:1-2; Mt 5:48
Catechism - #901, 915

WEEKLY OVERVIEW:
The readings discuss the need to strive for perfection for the sanctification of souls, the importance of speaking on the mercy of God, and some of the reflections of St. Faustina's meditations.

LEARNING AND DISCUSSION:
1) In *Diary* entry #1165, Jesus tells her of the need to strive for perfection for the sanctification of souls. It is said that to overcome a fault one should try to develop the virtue that corresponds with that fault.

If pride is a problem, then strive for humility. What are small things you can do daily to overcome a fault?

2) Discuss *Diary* entry #1167 in relation to the times we live, and describe ways in which we can better speak of God's mercy.

3) St. Faustina mentions how Jesus treated His enemies. Reflect on ways since the last meeting that you acted out of goodness, kindness, understanding and helping those in need.

LESSON GOALS:

At the end of the discussion, members should understand:
- The need to speak about Divine Mercy.
- Our continued need for hope and trust in striving for perfection.
- How we can better emulate Jesus in our relationships with others.

WEEK 120 — Read Diary quotes on forgiveness (#390, 723, 1148)

ADDITIONAL READING ASSIGNMENT TO PREPARE FOR THIS WEEK:

Scripture - Mk 11:25; Lk 15:11-32

Catechism - #2840

WEEKLY OVERVIEW:

The need for forgiveness and how it opens the door to Divine Mercy is discussed. The importance of living the Divine Mercy message daily through forgiveness cannot be overemphasized.

LEARNING AND DISCUSSION:

1) Whom do we resemble most when we forgive our neighbor? (*Diary*, 1148)

2) What are the greatest obstacles to holiness? (and explain why) (*Diary*, 1488)

3) Discuss situations in life where we are called to be like the Father in the story of the Prodigal Son.

LESSON GOALS:

At the end of the discussion, members should understand:
- That lack of forgiveness is a detriment to spiritual growth.

- Forgiveness is critical if we are to live the message of mercy.
- Anxiety and discouragement are obstacles to holiness.

WEEK 121 — Read the article on "Purgatory"
ADDITIONAL READING ASSIGNMENT TO PREPARE FOR THIS WEEK:
Scripture - Heb 12:14; 2 Tim 4:19; 2 Mac 12:42-46
Catechism - #1030
WEEKLY OVERVIEW:
The reality of purgatory, including Church teaching on the subject, is the topic for the week.
LEARNING AND DISCUSSION:
1) Why do we pray for the poor souls?
2) How do we think of loved ones whom might be in purgatory now?
3) How does the existence of purgatory manifest both the Justice and the Merciful Love of God?
LESSON GOALS:
At the end of the discussion, members should understand:
- Church teaching on purgatory.
- The importance of praying for the Poor Souls in purgatory.

WEEK 122 — *Diary*, 1210-1225
ADDITIONAL READING ASSIGNMENT TO PREPARE FOR THIS WEEK:
Scripture - Luke 15:1-7
Catechism - #2089
WEEKLY OVERVIEW:
The readings focus on the Novena to The Divine Mercy.
LEARNING AND DISCUSSION:
1) Discuss the importance of each individual group Our Lord asks St. Faustina to include in the novena.
2) What does the Church say about schismatics? (Catechism #2089)
3) How can we be included in the souls who especially venerate and glorify His mercy? (seventh day) How does St. Faustina describe such a soul?

LESSON GOALS:

At the end of the discussion, members should understand:

- That although the novena seems to have been intended primarily for St. Faustina's use, Our Lord must have wanted others to recite it as St. Faustina wrote it in her *Diary*.

WEEK 123 — *Diary*, 1226-1230

ADDITIONAL READING ASSIGNMENT TO PREPARE FOR THIS WEEK:

Scripture - 2 Mac 12:46

Catechism - #1030-1032

WEEKLY OVERVIEW:

The last two days of the Novena are the main themes.

LEARNING AND DISCUSSION:

1) What does Sacred Scripture (2 Maccabees 12:46) tell us about praying for the souls in purgatory? What does the Catholic Catechism say?
2) What is the significance of Our Lord including "lukewarm souls" in the Novena. Have we grown "lukewarm" in some areas?
3) How do our hopes and dreams of the day we shall see God compare to St. Faustina's? (*Diary*, 1230)

LESSON GOALS:

At the end of the discussion, members should understand:

- The importance of maintaining our fervor and zeal for the Lord, never becoming lukewarm in the faith.
- The importance of praying for the Poor Souls in purgatory.

WEEK 124 — Read Diary quotes on Mercy (#301, 367, 723, 1273, 1488)

ADDITIONAL READING ASSIGNMENT TO PREPARE FOR THIS WEEK:

Scripture - Mt 22:34-40; Is 29:13; Mt 5:20

Catechism - #1829, 2447

WEEKLY OVERVIEW:

The importance of being vessels of mercy, and living the message through the spiritual and corporal works of mercy are discussed.

LEARNING AND DISCUSSION:

1) What is mercy?
2) In what ways have we done works of mercy since last meeting?
3) Discuss spiritual works of mercy, and *Diary* entry #1317.

LESSON GOALS:

At the end of the discussion, members should understand:

- Mercy is the greatest attribute of God
- How we are to be vessels of mercy

WEEK 125 — *Diary*, 1231-1244

ADDITIONAL READING ASSIGNMENT TO PREPARE FOR THIS WEEK:

Scripture - Mt 7:7-11; Mt 10:26-28; Rev 12:1-6
Catechism - #963, 497-498, 511

WEEKLY OVERVIEW:

The Holy Eucharist, Our Blessed Mother, and the importance of trying to do God's will are the main topics discussed.

LEARNING AND DISCUSSION:

1) Why is it hard to reflect God's love to our enemies?
2) What virtues did Our Lady encourage in the vision of St. Faustina?
3) Do we allow God's presence in the Eucharist to affect us in the same way as it did St. Faustina?

LESSON GOALS:

At the end of the discussion, members should understand:

- The Eucharist unites us with God in a special way.
- The importance of doing God's will in our lives.
- Mary is a loving, protective mother.

WEEK 126 — *Diary*, 1245-1264

ADDITIONAL READING ASSIGNMENT TO PREPARE FOR THIS WEEK:

Scripture - Mt 27:45-46; Heb 12:5-13
Catechism - #1508

WEEKLY OVERVIEW:

The need for trust and trying to live in God's will are the major themes for discussion. The feeling of abandonment during times of trial is also mentioned.

LEARNING AND DISCUSSION:

1) Why does "an extraordinary fear" pervade St. Faustina's soul? (*Diary*, 1263)
2) Discuss the importance of doing things out of love. Do we do things at home and work out of love or obligation? (*Diary*, 1249)
3) Discuss the importance of realizing and submission to God's will.
4) Why does Our Lord tell St. Faustina that He was with her more in times of perceived abandonment than when she experienced ecstasy?

LESSON GOALS:

At the end of the discussion, members should understand:

- The importance of spiritual direction and a better understanding of the will of God.
- The importance of keeping our eyes on God, especially in times of trial.

WEEK 127 — *Diary*, 1265-1276

ADDITIONAL READING ASSIGNMENT TO PREPARE FOR THIS WEEK:

Scripture - Mt 8:18-22; Mt 23:1-7; Jon 4:10-11
Catechism - #1367-68, 1395, 1521, 2271

WEEKLY OVERVIEW:

We can offer up our sufferings with love and submission to God's will. Others will persecute and judge us, but great peace is attained through abandonment to the will of God. We can offer our sufferings up for those who persecute us, and for the work of the ministry. God's mercy is unfathomable, and we will never comprehend it.

LEARNING AND DISCUSSION:

1) What does the Lord promise to provide to Saint Faustina? (*Diary*, 1267)
2) When, how, and what special union does she feel with Jesus? (*Diary*, 1264)
3) What are the paradoxes of the granting of mercy? (*Diary*, 1273 & 1275)
4) How do St. Faustina's voluminous writings compare to God's mercy? (*Diary*, 1273)

5) What reparation is offered through St. Faustina's sufferings? (*Diary*, 1276)

LESSON GOALS:

At the end of the discussion, members should understand:

- How the greatest sinners can receive mercy.
- How suffering is beneficial for ourselves and others.
- The Church's teachings on the sanctity of all human life.

WEEK 128 — *Diary*, 1277-1293

ADDITIONAL READING ASSIGNMENT TO PREPARE FOR THIS WEEK:

Scripture - Jn 13:12-15; Jn 13:34-35
Catechism - #1996-97, 2004-2005

WEEKLY OVERVIEW:

St. Faustina's attitude and love for the less fortunate, her knowledge of God, souls with hardened hearts, religious vocations, and humility are topics for discussion.

LEARNING AND DISCUSSION:

1) In *Diary* entry #1279, Saint Faustina writes of a knowledge of the graces God was lavishing on her. Discuss situations in life where you felt an infusion of God's knowledge and graces.

2) In *Diary* entry #1282, she writes of her treatment of the poor. What are some of the frustrations in dealing with the poor? ? Have you encountered any souls like those described in entry #1284

3) In *Diary* entry #1293, the Lord speaks on weakness and humility. Why is a personal relationship with Jesus, and frequent participation in the Sacrament of Reconciliation so important?

LESSON GOALS:

At the end of the discussion, members should understand:

- The need for a personal relationship with Jesus.
- The importance of forgiveness.
- The importance of loving ourselves and those around us, and how we are to be vessels of mercy.

53

WEEK 129 — *Diary*, 1294-1309

ADDITIONAL READING ASSIGNMENT TO PREPARE FOR THIS WEEK:
Scripture - Lk 18:9-14; Jn 13:3-5, 12-15
Catechism - #2012-2013, 2016, 2540

WEEKLY OVERVIEW:
The topics discussed include the difficulties in life, lives of the saints, and the role of humility.

LEARNING AND DISCUSSION:
1) What did the Lord tell her about the trials and difficulties in life? (*Diary*, 1295) Does the saying "Do your best, let God do the rest" seem appropriate?
2) What did the saints say to St. Faustina about life on earth, and what was her reply? (*Diary*, 1304) How can we apply this to our daily struggles?
3) What is humility? How does she describe a humble soul? Reflect on ways since the last meeting in which you could have been more humble.

LESSON GOALS:
At the end of the discussion, members should understand:
- The importance of daily turning over to Jesus our struggles and tribulations.
- How the saints who preceded us left us examples of virtue and good counsel.

WEEK 130 — *Diary*, 1310-1321

ADDITIONAL READING ASSIGNMENT TO PREPARE FOR THIS WEEK:
Scripture - Mt 9:13; Lk 10:30-34; Jas 2:13
Catechism - #1700, 1930, 2276

WEEKLY OVERVIEW:
The topics for the week include our daily trials and how God rewards for the effort, the necessity of love for the poor and respect for all human life, and trying to do God's will.

LEARNING AND DISCUSSION:
1) Will we be rewarded for the greatness of our works? (*Diary*, 1310)
2) What is the lesson to be learned from *Diary* entries #1312 and 1317?

3) What did St. Faustina mean when she wrote, "Some are under the rule of love, others under the rule of justice?" (*Diary*, 1315) What rule do you live under?

LESSON GOALS:

At the end of the discussion, members should understand:
- God rewards for the effort and not the result.
- The power of the spiritual works of mercy.
- How we are to live under the rule of love.

WEEK 131 — *Diary*, 1322-1333

ADDITIONAL READING ASSIGNMENT TO PREPARE FOR THIS WEEK:

Scripture - Mt 10:12-14; Jn 14:27; Gal 5:22

Catechism - #736, 1832, 1731-1734

WEEKLY OVERVIEW:

The themes discussed include the struggle for inner peace amid life's turmoils, the need to forgive and ask God for forgiveness, and free will.

LEARNING AND DISCUSSION:

1) St. Faustina sailed peacefully amidst the roaring waves. How was she able to do that? (*Diary*, 1322)

2) What was her desire to get out of the retreat she attended? (*Diary*, 1326)

3) In *Diary* entry #1332, St. Faustina writes, "...forgive me every time that I ask your forgiveness with a contrite heart." Does God allot only a certain number of pardons? (*Diary*, 1488)

LESSON GOALS:

At the end of the discussion, members should understand:
- We should turn our difficulties over to Him, as He is the source of inner peace.
- The importance of forgiveness, that is, the need to forgive ourselves and others.
- How God's mercy is ours for the asking.

WEEK 132 — *Diary*, 1334-1354

ADDITIONAL READING ASSIGNMENT TO PREPARE FOR THIS WEEK:
Scripture - Mt 10:34-39
Catechism - #1457-1458

WEEKLY OVERVIEW:
Readings focus on sacrifice and the abundant grace God gives us to endure those sacrifices. St. Faustina felt great pain in knowing, while involuntarily, she had caused another soul pain.

LEARNING AND DISCUSSION:
1) When we feel abandoned and alone, how can we pick up our cross and carry on with our lives?
2) Reflecting on this past week, is there anyone to whom you caused pain? What ways can you try to atone for the suffering you caused that soul(s)?

LESSON GOALS:
At the end of the discussion, members should understand:
- God gives an abundance of grace to the soul of whom He is demanding sacrifice.
- God is truly present in the Eucharist and it should be paramount that we receive Him worthily, through the frequent reception of the Sacrament of Reconciliation.

WEEK 133 — *Diary*, 1355-1372

ADDITIONAL READING ASSIGNMENT TO PREPARE FOR THIS WEEK:
Scripture - Jn 14:1-4; Jn 14:25-31
Catechism - #956, 957

WEEKLY OVERVIEW:
This segment dealt with St. Faustina's attending a silent retreat. Readings highlight God's pleasure and outpouring of abundant grace and opportunity for those striving to become saints. As He did with St. Faustina, Jesus can give us the grace of suffering in order to use us as the instrument of another's conversion.

LEARNING AND DISCUSSION:
1) When was the last time you made a retreat or attended a Catholic conference? Pray for enlightenment from the Holy Spirit as to what retreat/conference you

should attend, committing as St. Faustina did, "to be thoroughly transformed by God's love."

2) St. Faustina had ideas on thanking God after returning from her retreat. Yet, she sought the advice of her spiritual director in order to "make all this more pleasing in the eyes of God and to remove the least shadow of doubt from her mind." Do you have a spiritual director? What advice would you ask of him?

LESSON GOALS:

At the end of the discussion, members should understand:

- The great value of a retreat as a source of renewing the soul, through God's great love and mercy.
- The importance of striving for Sainthood; as St. Faustina said, "to love God with a love so great that there would be no soul who has hitherto loved Him so."

WEEK 134 — *Diary,* 1373-1391

ADDITIONAL READING ASSIGNMENT TO PREPARE FOR THIS WEEK:

Scripture - 1 Cor 3:15; 1 Pet 1:7; 2 Macc 12:46
Catechism - #164, 1031-1032

WEEKLY OVERVIEW:

The themes of the week include praying for the dead, the importance of spreading the Divine Mercy message, purgatory, and reception of Holy Communion.

LEARNING AND DISCUSSION:

1) Did Saint Faustina pray for the dead? (*Diary,* 1375) Is this Church teaching? (*Catechism* #164)

2) Discuss the relevance and importance of praying the Chaplet, as well as the graces from the Image (*Diary,* 1379).

3) Discuss Holy Communion and *Diary* entry #1385.

LESSON GOALS:

At the end of the discussion, members should understand:

- The importance of praying for the dead and the poor souls in purgatory.
- The importance of evangelization of the Divine Mercy message, and the graces received from the image.

Week 135 — *Diary*, 1392-1409

ADDITIONAL READING ASSIGNMENT TO PREPARE FOR THIS WEEK:
Scripture - Col 1:24; Mt 16:24; Rom 12:1; 2 Cor 4:17-18
Catechism - #1508, 1521

WEEKLY OVERVIEW:
Suffering and inner peace amidst turmoil, living the faith, and evangelization of the message are themes for the group.

LEARNING AND DISCUSSION:
1) How does St. Faustina say that God's will shall be fulfilled in us?
2) Did suffering take away St. Faustina's peace? Did the peace lessen her suffering? (*Diary*, 1394)
3) How can we reassure sinners? (*Diary*, 1396)
4) Discuss *Diary* entry #1405. Have you ever had similar feelings, thoughts, or experiences?

LESSON GOALS:
At the end of the discussion, members should understand:
- The beauty of suffering and the desire for inner peace.
- How we can reassure even the greatest sinner.
- The importance of evangelization of the mercy of God.

Week 136 — *Diary*, 1410-1427

ADDITIONAL READING ASSIGNMENT TO PREPARE FOR THIS WEEK:
Scripture - Jn 15:1-9; Mt 28:20
Catechism - #208, 1088, 1373, 2144

WEEKLY OVERVIEW:
The writings focus on the awareness of the presence of God through faith, worship and devotion.

LEARNING AND DISCUSSION:
1) How aware are we of God's presence in our lives?
2) Is the presence of God an abstract truth or a living reality in my life?
3) How can I reflect His presence in my life as a Christian?

58

4) Discuss the different ways Christ is present to us through faith (intangible) and real presence (tangible).

5) What are the various ways that St. Faustina experiences the presence of God? (*Diary,* 844, 890, 1499)

LESSON GOALS:

At the end of the discussion, members should understand:
- Man's consciousness of the presence of God through faith and the sacraments.
- The effect of this consciousness on spiritual growth.

WEEK 137 — *Diary,* 1428-1443

ADDITIONAL READING ASSIGNMENT TO PREPARE FOR THIS WEEK:

Scripture - 1 Cor 1:18; 2 Cor 12:7-10; Jn 16:34;
Ps 50:15; Sir 2:1

Catechism - #1508, 1521

WEEKLY OVERVIEW:

The writings focus on the sufferings of St. Faustina and how she united her suffering to God for the sake of souls.

LEARNING AND DISCUSSION:

1) How did St. Faustina feel about the decay of her body? (*Diary,* 1428)

2) How do we feel about our own body?

3) Will death be a tragedy for her? (*Diary,* 1735) for us?

4) How does St. Faustina respond to the daily trials and tribulations that caused so much suffering in her life? (*Diary,* 1443)

LESSON GOALS:

At the end of the discussion, members should understand:
- The ways we respond to the sufferings we endure in our lives.
- How we unite our sufferings to the passion of Christ.
- How we rely on God's grace to bring us through difficult situations.

WEEK 138 — *Diary*, 1444-1457

ADDITIONAL READING ASSIGNMENT TO PREPARE FOR THIS WEEK:
Scripture - Ps 6:9-10; Jer 2:3-7; 2 Cor 2:1-11; Jas 5:16
Catechism - #363, 368, 2842-44

WEEKLY OVERVIEW:

This week's reading deals with Saint Faustina's torments of loneliness, physical and moral sufferings, and how the Lord puts it in perspective for her, leading to a greater appreciation of suffering and growth through it.

LEARNING AND DISCUSSION:

1) What no longer surprises Saint Fausina? What is it that people do not know how to perceive?
2) What pains the Lord? To what does He liken His pain?
3) Where is solace to be found?
4) What did St. Faustina experience when she spiritually went to the Tabernacle and cried?

LESSON GOALS:

At the end of the discussion, members should understand:

- The Lord (not humans) understands our heart and He (not humans) will ultimately judge us.
- The miracle that is the Sacrament of Reconciliation.
- Praying for our enemies brings peace and also unity with our fellow Christians.

WEEK 139 — *Diary*, 1458-1478

ADDITIONAL READING ASSIGNMENT TO PREPARE FOR THIS WEEK:
Scripture - Zech 3:1-2; Prov 18:14; 2 Cor 3:6; Col 1:24-27
Catechism - #309, 395, 8126, 1889

WEEKLY OVERVIEW:

This week's reading deals with the Lord showing St. Faustina how giving power to human murmurings distances us from Him and how praying for sinners disgusts the Evil One and drives him away, if we persevere. The Lord also reveals the importance of love over intellect.

LEARNING AND DISCUSSION:

1) What did Jesus reveal to St. Faustina that she did that gave the sisters greater cause for murmuring.

2) How did St. Faustina rebuke Satan while she prayed?
3) What struck St. Faustina during First Friday Mass?
4) Why does St. Faustina ask for a greater intellect?
5) What saddens Jesus?

LESSON GOALS:
> At the end of the discussion, members should understand:
> - Satan uses the murmurs of others to try to distance us from God.
> - Prayer for sinners and offerings of sufferings for them can release them from Satan's clutches.
> - Suffering can ultimately produce peace.
> - The grace of greater intellect is valuable when used for greater knowledge of the Lord.
> - Our everyday movements, gestures, etc. can greatly influence others.
> - Our reliance on the letter, rather than love, saddens Jesus.

WEEK 140 — *Diary*, 1479-1486

ADDITIONAL READING ASSIGNMENT TO PREPARE FOR THIS WEEK:
> Scripture - Ps 56; Ps 28:3-7; 2 Cor 4:3-6
> Catechism - #410, 598

WEEKLY OVERVIEW:
> This week's lesson deals with St. Faustina's inner conflict between the knowledge that God will protect her from the darkness of evil and the fear that she may be contributing to that evil with her own sin.

LEARNING AND DISCUSSION:
> 1) Why did Jesus take the appearance of a little child to commune with St. Faustina?
> 2) Why did the sin of "lack of trust" wound the heart of Jesus more than any other sin?
> 3) How does Jesus give us strength in our own daily struggles?

LESSON GOALS:
> At the end of the discussion, members should understand:
> - The importance of accepting that God loves us.
> - That as Our Father and Husband to His Bride, the Church, He protects those He loves.

- The importance of relying on God's immeasurable strength to shield His children.

WEEK 141 — *Diary*, 1487-1488
ADDITIONAL READING ASSIGNMENT TO PREPARE FOR THIS WEEK:
Scripture - Ps 46:11-12; Mt 5:10-11
Catechism - #164, 165, 1508
WEEKLY OVERVIEW:
This week's lesson deals with Jesus embracing Faustina in His loving arms and encouraging her to tell Him all her troubles, as a friend would.
LEARNING AND DISCUSSION:
1) How can we draw strength from receiving communion frequently?
2) Why does God allow suffering and persecution?
3) How can we glorify God with our sufferings?
LESSON GOALS:
At the end of the discussion, members should understand:
- The importance of prayer and talking to Jesus as a friend.
- Why we should not rely so heavily on other people.

WEEK 142 — *Diary*, 1489-1494
ADDITIONAL READING ASSIGNMENT TO PREPARE FOR THIS WEEK:
Scripture - Is 12; Ps 131; Rom 11:30-36
Catechism - #27
WEEKLY OVERVIEW:
This week's lesson chronicles the Conversation of the Merciful God with a Perfect Soul. The soul desires only to praise and adore God, most especially through the sacrament of Holy Communion. Jesus is pleased with the soul, "more than the angelic chorus," and reminds the soul to always trust completely in Him.
LEARNING AND DISCUSSION:
1) When I pray, do I focus on my needs, my pain, my wants, and my unhappiness, or do I spend the vast majority of my prayer time in thanksgiving and adoration?

2) Do I trust in God, as the Perfect Soul did, even when I don't feel completely restored from doing so?

Lesson Goals:

At the end of the discussion, members should understand:

- The sole purpose of prayer is to thank, praise, and adore God.
- While on Earth, not even the Perfect Soul feels perfect at all times. We must give ourselves completely to God, but we will still suffer for what we believe.
- To the same extent that we trust in God, will He be merciful unto us.
- Feeling both complete darkness and complete goodness is a chief characteristic of the Perfect Soul. Only a lukewarm soul would never feel complete darkness, but he would also never feel complete goodness.

Week 143 — *Diary*, 1495-1509

Additional Reading Assignment to Prepare For This Week:

Scripture - Mt 26:36-46; Lk 4:1-13
Catechism - #1763-1766

Weekly Overview:

The closer Saint Faustina grew to the Lord, the more Satan tempted her. But in choosing not to respond to Satan's deceitful comments, Faustina grew stronger in the Lord.

Learning and Discussion:

1) When a brother or sister who is not in Christ tempts me with empty words, do I get lost in argument with him or her or do I turn it over to God?
2) When I perform the Works of Mercy, do I help only in ways I am comfortable with, or do I assist the "lepers" of society for whom nobody else would otherwise defend.

Lesson Goals:

At the end of the discussion, members should understand:

- Help the neglected of society, especially in those cases that make us most uncomfortable.

- If Satan enters our minds, we should not panic – it is a sign that we are doing good, because Satan spends time only trying to weaken the body.
- We should always be completely honest and open with our confessor (s).

WEEK 144 — *Diary*, 1510-1532

ADDITIONAL READING ASSIGNMENT TO PREPARE FOR THIS WEEK:

Scripture - 2 Tim 2:11-13; 1 Pet 4:12-19; Jude 1:20-23
Catechism – #1994, 2010-2011

WEEKLY OVERVIEW:

Through St. Faustina, we consider the value of our sufferings united with our Master's sorrowful Passion. Jesus holds back the just anger of the Father by His mercy and invites us to approach the depths of it to attain justification, be strengthened, and to attain divine peace at the hour of death. Proclaiming His mercy draws down blessings, especially for priests. Trusting in His mercy and trusting in His will completely is His desire for us.

LEARNING AND DISCUSSION:

1) How should we treat our suffering(s) if we are disciples of the Crucified Master? (*Diary*, 1512)
2) How do the Lord's words in *Diary* entry #1532 contrast His invitation to trust in His mercy?
3) How would a priest enrich his ministry by promoting the Divine Mercy? (*Diary*, 1521) How can I refresh the heart of Jesus in my home, school, or workplace? Do I trust Him, His will above my own, to the last detail as He asks? (*Diary*, 1531)

LESSON GOALS:

At the end of the discussion, members should understand:

- The promises Jesus makes to those who promote and trust in His mercy and loving will completely.
- Even our suffering can be of infinite value when entrusted to His merciful will and sorrowful Passion.

64

WEEK 145 — *Diary*, 1533-1552
ADDITIONAL READING ASSIGNMENT TO PREPARE FOR THIS WEEK:
Scripture - 2 Cor 4:1
Catechism - #1731
WEEKLY OVERVIEW:
The Lord tells St. Faustina that He will grant everything a
soul asks of Him by saying the chaplet, and if the
chaplet is said in the presence of the dying, He will
stand between His Father and the dying, not as a just
judge but as the merciful Savior.
LEARNING AND DISCUSSION:
1) What does the Lord promise to souls who will glorify
His mercy and spread its worship? How can you do
this at work? (*Diary*, 1540)
2) In what way does St. Faustina accept everything that
comes her way (*Diary*, 1540) by the will of God?
(*Diary*, 1549)
3) In cases of doubt, what does St. Faustina do? (*Diary*,
1556)
LESSON GOALS:
At the end of the discussion, members should understand:
- How spreading the message of Divine Mercy will
obtain many graces for ourselves and for others.
- That by cooperating with God's grace and
doing His will we will give God the glory he
expects of us.

WEEK 146 — *Diary*, 1553-1565
ADDITIONAL READING ASSIGNMENT TO PREPARE FOR THIS WEEK:
Scripture - 2 Mac 6:16; Bar 3:2; Lk 8:50; Neh 9:31
Catechism - #741, 2756
WEEKLY OVERVIEW:
Topics for the week include God's incomprehensible
Mercy - Chosen Souls like St. Faustina and real
humiliation.
LEARNING AND DISCUSSION:
1) Sometimes He disciplines us with misfortunes, but
does He ever withdraw His mercy from us?
2) Are some souls chosen souls? Do they receive more

grace than the average soul?

3) How can we grow in real humility?

LESSON GOALS:

At the end of the discussion, members should understand:

- We are called to proclaim His mercy and if a soul does not exercise mercy, somehow or other, it will not obtain His mercy on the day of judgement.
- Temptations give you a chance to show your fidelity to God.
- Some souls are especially chosen, and whom He calls to a higher form of holiness. God demands greater love than He does from others. It's a special call, but the soul may either follow this call or not.

WEEK 147 — *Diary*, 1566-1580

ADDITIONAL READING ASSIGNMENT TO PREPARE FOR THIS WEEK:

Scripture - Lk 7:44-49; Lk 23:44-49; John 19:33-36

Catechism - #2304-5, 2447

WEEKLY OVERVIEW:

The chaplet is a very important tool that appeases the anger of God. It may be the only hope of salvation for certain souls. We are to expect to obtain everything promised us by Jesus. The hour of great grace for the whole world is the 3 o'clock hour where mercy triumphed over justice.

LEARNING AND DISCUSSION:

1) How does trust play a part in the mercy we receive? How can you tell others?

2) How is God's mercy greater than our worst sin?

3) Why do we need to meditate on His passion to better understand His mercy?

LESSON GOALS:

At the end of the discussion, members should understand:

- The need to trust in God's mercy – to receive His graces He has for us.
- The need to believe in His promises – "Trust in His mercy."
- God desires obedience, humility and trust to receive His mercy.

WEEK 148 — *Diary*, 1581-1589

ADDITIONAL READING ASSIGNMENT TO PREPARE FOR THIS WEEK:

Scripture - Ps 50; Rom 8:17; Col. 3:5; Jn 7:20

Catechism - #1430-1439

Diary quotes - #1031, 1318, 1295

WEEKLY OVERVIEW:

The readings reflect on doing God's will, just as the Blessed Mother had done. Even when she was joyful, she kept her eyes fixed on the cross. Mary's life was a practice of mortification.

LEARNING AND DISCUSSION:

1) True love is carrying out God's will. How do we discern God's will?

2) Why does interior mortification take place over practicing exterior mortification?

LESSON GOALS:

At the end of the discussion, members should understand:

- God calls each one of us to conversion and penance; conversion of the heart (interior mortification). This urges us on to gestures: taking up one's cross every day to follow Christ Crucified (exterior mortification).
- The importance of fasting, prayer and thanksgiving.

WEEK 149 — *Diary*, 1590-1608

ADDITIONAL READING ASSIGNMENT TO PREPARE FOR THIS WEEK:

Scripture - Jude 17:23

Catechism - #1846-1848

Diary quotes - #848, 1320, 1142

WEEKLY OVERVIEW:

God reveals to St. Faustina her assignment and duty "to beg for mercy for the whole world." He makes her the administrator of His mercy – **No soul will be justified until it turns with confidence to My mercy and that is why the first Sunday after Easter is to be the Feast of Mercy.**

LEARNING AND DISCUSSION:

1) Even in the smallest imperfections, God is merciful. What action of grace moves us to seek His consolation?

2) **The greater the sinner, the greater My mercy.**

St. Faustina wrote in her *Diary* that the world would know God's mercy. How are we to reach those who have not read the *Diary* or know about Divine Mercy Sunday? (*Diary*,1146)

LESSON GOALS:

At the end of the discussion, members should understand:

- The importance of spreading Divine Mercy on the Feast of Mercy and every day.
- "Let us take time for mercy while there is still time for mercy."

WEEK 150 — *Diary*, 1609-1629

ADDITIONAL READING ASSIGNMENT TO PREPARE FOR THIS WEEK:

Scripture - 1 Pet 1:6-8; 1 Pet 4:1-6 & 12-19; Pet 3:14-18; Col 1:24, 25; 2 Cor 4:16-18

Catechism - #1508, 1521

WEEKLY OVERVIEW:

There is strength in suffering. The Lord teaches St. Faustina (and ourselves) more about suffering – the fruit of it and the spiritual attitude towards it.

LEARNING AND DISCUSSION:

1) How does St. Faustina model her experience after the Lord's? (*Diary*, 1609)
2) How does this relationship give us strength in trials/sufferings? (1 Peter 1:4)
3) What was the key to St. Faustina's attitude toward suffering? (*Diary*, 1612-1613, 1620)
4) What is reparation? (Col 1:24-25) Am I willing to enroll in the "Lord's School" (*Diary*, 1626-1628)?
5) What is His formula for discerning the love in one's suffering?

LESSON GOALS:

At the end of the discussion, members should understand:

- We should know the gospel dimension to "redemptive suffering" and the fruits of union with the Passion of Jesus.
- Experience the soul's source of strength – Jesus — during time of human weakness.

68

- Pray for the triumph of the merciful heart
  through our trials, sufferings, annoyances and
  contradictions.

WEEK 151 — *Diary*, 1630-1638
ADDITIONAL READING ASSIGNMENT TO PREPARE FOR THIS WEEK:
Scripture - Rom 12:1-2; Heb 11:13-16; Col. 3:1-3
Catechism - #2825, 2642, 1026-1029
WEEKLY OVERVIEW:
St. Faustina praises and trusts God despite severe
physical torments from tuberculosis. She also suffers
misunderstanding and even moral suffering – all for
souls, as her gift to Jesus.
LEARNING AND DISCUSSION:
1) Discuss the ways she (and the faithful) considered
   herself to be like a Host, in her Hymn of praise.
   How can you be a Host at work and home?
2) St. Faustina felt herself to be a royal child, in exile
   (*Diary*, 1632). How do I also feel that my heart's
   home is not of this world?
3) How did St. Faustina claim peace throughout her
   agonies? (*Diary*, 1635, 1637) [a key in last sentence]
LESSON GOALS:
At the end of the discussion, members should understand:
- We should focus not on our difficulties, but in
  God's plan.
- The difference between the "spirit" and the "letter"
  of our spirituality when difficulties or trials arise.

WEEK 152 — *Diary*, 1639-1653

ADDITIONAL READING ASSIGNMENT TO PREPARE FOR THIS WEEK:
Scripture - Gen 4:13; Mt 27:3-5
Catechism - #2091-2092

WEEKLY OVERVIEW:
The need to ask for God's mercy, the sin of presumption, Sister's desire to be a saint, and grace are topics discussed.

LEARNING AND DISCUSSION:
1) What obstruct's God's grace? (*Diary*, 1641)
2) Should we worry about adversity? (*Diary*, 1647)
3) What is the sin of despair? Of presumption?

LESSON GOALS:
At the end of the discussion, members should understand:
- The role of sin in obstructing grace.
- Suffering and the role of adversity.
- The sin of despair and presumption.

WEEK 153 — *Diary*, 1654-1667

ADDITIONAL READING ASSIGNMENT TO PREPARE FOR THIS WEEK:
Scripture - Wis 3:3-6; Lk 24:36; Gal 5:22
Catechism - #1829, 2305

WEEKLY OVERVIEW:
The need for peace amidst trials, the need for understanding so as to better understand His mercy, and the way St. Faustina handled her sufferings are topics discussed.

LEARNING AND DISCUSSION:
1) What did St. Faustina say she needed to lean on to get through life? (*Diary*, 1654) What do we often use to lean on instead?
2) What did she acquire by meditating on His Passion? (*Diary*, 1657)
3) What was the delight of her heart? (*Diary*, 1662)

LESSON GOALS:
At the end of the discussion, members should understand:
- The desire for God's peace in our hearts.

- How God's mercy is unfathomable and ever-present.
- Suffering can bring us closer to God.

WEEK 154 — *Diary*, 1668-1682
ADDITIONAL READING ASSIGNMENT TO PREPARE FOR THIS WEEK:
Scripture - Phil 1:21-25; 4:6, 7; Ps 27:4-6
Catechism - #1368, 1546

WEEKLY OVERVIEW:
Topics discussed include the graces obtained from reception of Holy Communion, the celebration of the sacrifice of the Mass, and how we are to offer our lives and trials up to God.

LEARNING AND DISCUSSION:
1) How did St. Faustina prepare spiritually for Holy Communion? Discuss ways it was important to her.
2) How did St. Faustina offer up herself as a holocaust/sacrifice? What can I offer up to God to participate in the Pascal sacrifice?
3) In addition to the visit of the "Lord of Angels," what were her benefits in preparing for and receiving Holy Communion? (*Diary*, 1679)
4) Why did the Seraph answer her question of confession as he did? (*Diary*, 1677) Do I take this opportunity frequently enough?

LESSON GOALS:
At the end of the discussion, members should understand:
- The power of participating in Holy Mass by offering ourselves, our trials, hopes, and sufferings with the Eucharistic Sacrifice.
- The benefits of peace and joy, obtained by seeking God's will above our own.

WEEK 155 — *Diary*, 1683-1698

ADDITIONAL READING ASSIGNMENT TO PREPARE FOR THIS WEEK:

Scripture - Ps 81; Lk 5:43-48

Catechism - #863, 2096-7

WEEKLY OVERVIEW:

The Lord is speaking to us about the mission of mercy: to be receptive to His generous grace, to let go and entrust all things to His mercy; to win souls through prayer and sacrifice, encouraging them to approach Him, and to love even enemies for Him that His mercy will be reflected in us.

LEARNING AND DISCUSSION:

1) What pearls and diamonds from Jesus (*Diary*, 1687) do we neglect to pick up? How do we become receptive? (*Diary*, 1683)

2) What should we offer up to the Lord so as to achieve peace in our souls? (*Diary*, 1685)

3) Jesus commended Faustina for loving a difficult person in *Diary* entry #1694-1695, **Be merciful as I am merciful. Love everyone out of love for Me, even your greatest enemies, so that My mercy may be fully reflected in your heart.** Share some experiences by which you experienced this to be true.

LESSON GOALS:

At the end of the discussion, members should understand:

- God is calling us to give ourselves entirely to Himself so He can cleanse us, fulfill us, and make us vessels of mercy.
- The importance of prayer and sacrifice to save souls, and to encourage souls in our reach to have the same confidence and trust of God so as to receive the gems of His grace.
- The Lord's instructions for entrustment to His will and the peace we receive when we do so.

WEEK 156 — *Diary*, 1699-1711

ADDITIONAL READING ASSIGNMENT TO PREPARE FOR THIS WEEK:

Scripture - Mat 9:13; Mat 20:1-9; Rev 3:15-16;
1 Cor 13:3; 1 Jn 4:16; 1 Jn 5:2; Jn 16:13
Catechism - #220-221, 589, 733, 1826, 1829
(see St. Augustine's comments)

WEEKLY OVERVIEW:

Three main points cover this week's section. The first is that God's mercy is readily available, even up to the gates of hell. The second is the contrast of the lukewarm soul with that of the fervent love-filled soul of Saint Faustina. The third is God may directly instruct someone.

LEARNING AND DISCUSSION:

1) Why is God merciful even to the last moment of life?
2) How are the convents and churches described in the *Diary* entry #1702 like the church of Laodicea in Rev 3:14? What is different about St. Faustina and the others that is pleasing to Jesus?
3) How does God teach us?

LESSON GOALS:

At the end of the discussion, members should understand:
• That God is love and He desires to be merciful.
• To truly please God, we need to love and obey Him.

WEEK 157 — *Diary*, 1712-1728

ADDITIONAL READING ASSIGNMENT TO PREPARE FOR THIS WEEK:

Scripture - Lk 1:48; 51-53; Lk 18:9-14; Jas 5:16;
Rev 3:20; Eph 3:17
Catechism - #2014, 2559, 2613.

WEEKLY OVERVIEW:

One of the main points in this section is the contrast between humility and pride. A person steeped in pride is opposed by God (*Diary*, 1716 and 1717) but the humble are pleasing to Him. Saint Faustina's humility as seen in *Diary* entry #1727 greatly influences God's action (*Diary* 1713 & 1722). Her prayers of intercession are pleasing to God. Finally, we can see her great love of God hidden in the "fragile form of bread" and her constant invitation for Him to live in her heart.

LEARNING AND DISCUSSION:

1) Why is God pleased with the humble and opposed to the proud? Reflect on a recent incident where you could have been more humble.

2) Contrast *Diary* entry #1714 versus *Diary* entry #1722; why would God hold back on sending punishments on the whole earth but apply her prayers for her convent to other intentions?

3) How can we give Jesus our heart, so He can dwell there?

LESSON GOALS:

At the end of the discussion, members should understand:

- That God opposes the proud but listens to the humble.
- That God listens to the fervent prayer of a righteous person.
- That we should love God so much that we want Him to always dwell with us.

WEEK 158 — *Diary*, 1729-1742

ADDITIONAL READING ASSIGNMENT TO PREPARE FOR THIS WEEK:

Scripture - Job 13:15; Is 35:4; 2 Thess 1:10
Catechism - #1813, 1817-21, 2091

WEEKLY OVERVIEW:

In the readings, it is obvious that St. Faustina was prepared to die and knew her health was failing. However, she only wanted to do God's will. The *Diary* mentions a "spark coming from Poland" that will prepare the world for the final coming.

LEARNING AND DISCUSSION:

1) What was paramount to St. Faustina? (*Diary*, 1729)

2) What did God tell her about His relationship with a contrite soul? (*Diary*, 1739)

3) Can we pray for any intention when praying the Chaplet? (*Diary*, 1731)

LESSON GOALS:
At the end of the discussion, members should understand:
- Doing God's will is paramount.
- The need to trust in His mercy always.

WEEK 159 — *Diary*, 1743-1748
ADDITIONAL READING ASSIGNMENT TO PREPARE FOR THIS WEEK:
Scripture - Rev 11:19; Rev 12:1-6
Catechism - #1431, 1451
WEEKLY OVERVIEW:
The need for illumination of our souls so that we can understand God's love and mercy, as well as the Blessed Mother as a Tabernacle for Jesus, are topics discussed.
LEARNING AND DISCUSSION:
1) In God's goodness, what did He give us? (*Diary*, 1743)
2) What did St. Faustina ask the Lord to do in *Diary* entry #1744?
3) Who is the Ark of the Covenant?
LESSON GOALS:
At the end of the discussion, members should understand:
- The need for conversion in our lives.
- The need for God's mercy in our lives.
- The role of Our Lady as the Tabernacle of Mercy.

WEEK 160 — *Diary*, 1749-1760
ADDITIONAL READING ASSIGNMENT TO PREPARE FOR THIS WEEK:
Scripture - Jn 1:1-5; Eph 1:4-5
Catechism – #2473-2474
WEEKLY OVERVIEW:
The Lord Jesus asks St. Faustina to make a three day retreat. With the instructions "Do not be afraid," Jesus expresses to her His unending love for her, present before the beginning of the world and lasting for all eternity. Jesus also asks her to consider the "treasure of grace" that He grants her. She responds that she will pay more attention to the gift of grace and not upon the vessel that brought it to her. He tells St. Faustina to have

recourse with His most merciful heart when she experiences desolation and various doubts. She is to trust her spiritual director's advice for he speaks with the Lord's voice, and not to be afraid of struggle.

LEARNING AND DISCUSSION:

1) Why did St. Faustina ask her Superior's permission before attending the Retreat even though Jesus told her to participate?

2) How does Jesus tell St. Faustina to deal with temptations? (*Diary*, 1760)

3) How does St. Faustina resolve to receive "treasures of grace?" (*Diary*, 1759)

LESSON GOALS:

At the end of the discussion, members should understand:

- The importance of trust and obedience to those that God has placed above us in authority.
- We should accept grace regardless of the vessel that carries it.

WEEK 161 — *Diary*, 1761-1782

ADDITIONAL READING ASSIGNMENT TO PREPARE FOR THIS WEEK:

Scripture - Rom 5:6-11; 2 Cor 1:5; Mk 12:28-31
Catechism - #164-165

WEEKLY OVERVIEW:

The Lord Jesus asks St. Faustina to contemplate His Passion as if it were for her sake alone. Through this meditation, St. Faustina comes to the realization of the "great worth of the human soul and the great evil of sin." Jesus also reveals to St. Faustina how highly He values the rule and the vows of the religious, saying that through them He pours graces upon the religious. In addition, Jesus instructs St. Faustina in the importance of sacrifice and prayer, particularly for her neighbor. From His most Merciful Heart, graces flow out upon the whole world. Jesus commands her to pray especially for the dying, for they are in most need of trust, and have it the least.

LEARNING AND DISCUSSION:

1) What is the importance and significance of sacrifice and prayer?

2) Is your love for your neighbor "guided by My love?" (*Diary*, 1768)

3) Why do we need to strive for recollection in our souls?

LESSON GOALS:

At the end of the discussion, members should understand:

- Redemptive suffering and the importance of prayer, especially for our neighbors and the dying.
- Graces flow out upon the whole world from the Heart of Jesus.
- The importance of recollection for the soul so as to hear the voice of God.

WEEK 162 — *Diary*, 1783-1803

ADDITIONAL READING ASSIGNMENT TO PREPARE FOR THIS WEEK:

Scripture - Jn 14:6; Eph 2:8-9; 2 Thess 2:12

Catechism - #1521, 2636, 2653

WEEKLY OVERVIEW:

Our Lord's desire for the salvation of every soul; the role our sufferings and prayers can play in helping this cause, and our need to give of ourselves first, in every event and circumstance to Jesus' will and mercy for our own and the salvation of others.

LEARNING AND DISCUSSION:

1) St. Faustina was gifted with a great desire to save souls. How can we obtain this desire to a greater degree and how important is mercy in us for our salvation and theirs? (*Diary*, 1797)

2) In what ways can we obtain mercy for others and ourselves? (*Diary* 1791, 1797)

3) How important is our knowledge of our own misery and sinfulness to obtaining mercy? (*Diary*, 1802)

LESSON GOALS:

At the end of the discussion, members should understand:

- Our Lord's mercy related to His great love for us.
- How our sufferings and prayers can benefit our soul and the souls of others.

Made in the USA
Charleston, SC
14 June 2014